this
little ORCHARD

book belongs to

....

....

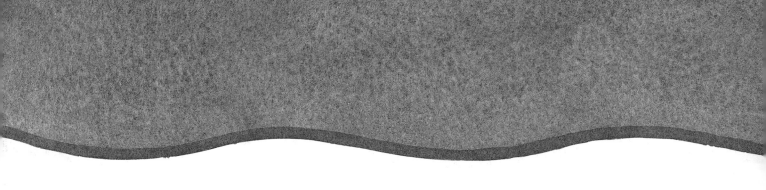

For Ellie and Luca

ORCHARD BOOKS
96 Leonard Street, London EC2A 4XD
Orchard Books Australia
Unit 31, 56 O'Riordan St, Alexandria, NSW 2015
1 84121 291 1 (hardback)
1 84121 293 8 (paperback)
First published in Great Britain in 2001
Copyright © Penny Dann 2001
The right of Penny Dann to be identified
as the author and illustrator of this work has been asserted by her
in accordance with the Copyright, Designs and Patents Act, 1988.
A CIP catalogue record for this book is available from the British Library.
1 3 5 7 9 10 8 6 4 2 (hardback)
1 3 5 7 9 10 8 6 4 2 (paperback)
Printed in Italy

If you're happy and you know it

Penny Dann

little ORCHARD

If you're happy and you know it,
clap your hands;
If you're happy and you know it,
clap your hands;

If you're happy and you know it
And you really want to show it,

If you're happy and you know it,
clap your hands.

If you're happy
and you know it,
stamp your feet;

If you're happy
and you know it,
stamp your feet;

If you're happy and you know it
And you really want to show it,

If you're happy and you know it,
stamp your feet.

If you're happy and you know it,
wave your hand;
If you're happy and you know it,
wave your hand;

If you're happy and you know it
And you really want to show it,

If you're happy and you know it,
wave your hand.

If you're happy
and you know it,
nod your head;

If you're happy
and you know it,
nod your head;

If you're happy and you know it
And you really want to show it,

If you're happy and you know it,
nod your head.

If you're happy and you know it,
touch your toes;
If you're happy and you know it,
touch your toes;

If you're happy and you know it
And you really want to show it,

If you're happy and you know it,
touch your toes.

If you're happy
and you know it,
swing your arms;

If you're happy
and you know it,
swing your arms;

If you're happy and you know it
And you really want to show it,

If you're happy and you know it,
swing your arms.

If you're happy
and you know it,
hop around;

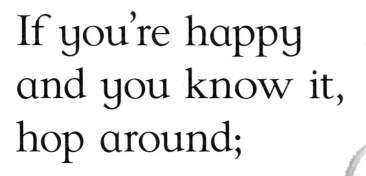

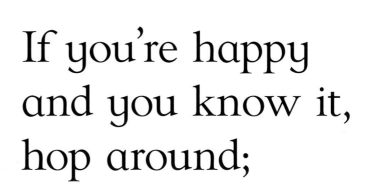

If you're happy
and you know it,
hop around;

If you're happy and you know it
And you really want to show it,

If you're happy and you know it,
hop around.

If you're happy and you know it,
shout "We are!"
If you're happy and you know it,
shout "We are!"

We are!

If you're happy and you know it
And you really want to show it,
If you're happy and you know it,
shout "We are!"

We are!